EX LIBRIS

ugly drawers, pretty panties

Tiffany Vakilian

www.awordwithyoupress.com

Vakilian, Tiffany
Ugly drawers, Pretty Panties

ISBN-13: 978-0-9843064-7-3

Ugly Drawers, Pretty Panties is published by: A Word with You Press

2023 Design by Speak Fire Publishing

For information please direct emails to:
info@speakfire.today or visit our website: www.speakfire.today

First Edition, June 2015

Printed in the United States of America

27 26 25 24 23   4 5 6 7 8

The praise keeps coming...

a collection
of poetry,
prose,
dreams and
missives

Tiffany Vakilian

PLEASE LEAVE A REVIEW!

affiliate link

Introduction

I come from storytellers.
Our history is such that our mundane happenings become performances in sharing with others.

One night, my brother reminded us how he wrapped his desktop computer in a pink woven blanket, secured that with duct tape (for handles) and took it on a plane to England, just to have it fry due to a faulty converter on his first plug-in to their 230-volt socket. The memory always made me smile, but last night's remindering lit my laugh muscles on fire for about five minutes. I'm still smoldering with hahaha's.

And so, for him (and some other people) - here is a reminder to tell your stories. I wrote this for all storytellers, griots, cantadoras and the like.

Find your chairs, your trees, your stages and platforms. Your audience is already listening, whether you see them or not. The sun is going down, and it is time.

TABLE OF CONTENTS

This One is for "SHE"   1

Tell Your Story   2

Untitled   3

Hindrances   4

Good Morning, I Don't Want to Write   5

Corporate Hierarchy Poetry for the VP
From the Executive Assistant   7

Breathing   9

I Wonder About My Fairy Folk   10

4/5/99   13

The House, The House, The House   14

Inside of me…   14

How Much?   15

When the Spirit Moves   16

Can I Sit Here?   17

I Am Sorry   18

See   20

Just   21

Who do I owe an apology to…   21

What is the Shape of Your Body?   22

The Whole You Naked   24

About My Nipples   25

My Violin of an Armpit   26

A Letter   26

My Thighs   27

Joints — 28

Cycle — 30

The Art of Shutting Up — 31

Our Cocoons — 33

Dreams and Maelstroms — 35

There is a coldness... — 35

Opaque Glass Houses — 36

Bloodlust — 37

Impact Tremors — 38

Can You Guess? — 39

Exquisite — 40

And just like that... — 40

Considering a Paradox — 41

Theme & Variations — 42

To Busboys and Poets — 45

Love can complete... — 45

One Dream in Prose — 47

I See Dying People — 48

I Was Considering… — 49

Harbinger — 50

dry souls — 51

"Yes dry souls do all of those things but why do they do those things?" — 52

Sometimes — 53

In the Desert — 54

Apologies 4 not 1 — 56

I have no inclinations…   56

Mirrors I   57

Untitled   58

On Display   59

Stain on My Shirt   60

Windows   61

Private Path, Locked Door   62

Mirrors II   63

Thoughts on   64

Coffee Colored Word Play   65

Note to the Fallen   66

On Self-amputation   67

Inspired by the Phrase I   67

Inspired by the Phrase II   68

Inspired by the Phrase III   69

A Sonnet on the Move   70

Of Anticipation   71

But Biding, I Live Beyond My Own Love   72

Satan and a Spot   76

The Difference   77

9-10-11   78

Redefining Family   79

I Want to Tell Them…   81

Blessed by blood and bone…   81

Things My Mama Says   82

Ugly Drawers, Pretty Panties   83

4c With A White Man 85

Maybe It's Just Me 86

Bravery 87

So Honored 88

I Look to You 89

Almost 90

Worlds 91

Cuando me sueño… 91

In Transit 92

Season 93

Pondering 94

At Any Age 95

Girl Thinks 96

For the Seiling Girls 97

The Contradictions 97

Two Weeks' Notice 98

Weeding Word Weeds 99

A Letter 100

We Chased Dragons 101

A Real Woman 102

A Woman but More 103

Too Strong to Bind 104

Rehearsing Victories 105

Time Capsule 106

For Moses.
And for Andrew.

With so much love.

ugly
drawers,
pretty
panties

This One Is for "SHE"

She is me
She is someone I've never met
She is my daughter, my mother, my home-girl
She is single
She is married
She is a prod-i-gal daughter
She is a princess
Her name is Mary
Her name is Martha
Her name is Michele
Her name is Kristy
Her name is Danica
Her name is Simone
Her name is "Appearance of God"
or "Song of Joy"
or "Bitter"
or "Desolate"
or she is not named at all
I want to tell her story
as I see it now, as I saw it then, as I dream it to be
with dots, and jots, and tittles
& mistakes
& false starts
and re-arrangings
as long as the story is told
as long as the perspective is expressed
as long as she knows
I see her
I know her
I love her

Tell Your Story

I say

Have the auDACity to tell your story ladies. Have the auDACity to tell your story. For those who don't have the ability to tell their stories, or, better yet, for those who do have the ability, but are terrified.

Who live daily, moment, second, millisecond so close every moment in their story. They can't breathe for the terror of the responsibility of holding that story.

Oh but it holds. It holds. It holds it holds… it holds. But for us. The storytellers. The storytellers. The storytellers. The stellar storytellers. We have the ability to tell our stories. And we are not silent. Even when we're quiet, we are not silent. When we don't speak, we yell bright yellow. Bright bright bright bright bright shiny stories just by existing.

Holding our stories. Knowing. Knowing we are holding the story. Know that we are holding a story. Knowing that we are holding a story for the voiceless ones that don't have a voice to tell the story – for the lazy ones who don't want to tell the story - for the terrified ones who can't tell the story.

We tell the story. We tell the story. We ARE the story. Our voice, a story. We tell our voice - a story. And give our stories voice.

Ladies tell your story. Ladies tell your story. Tell your gritty grimy nasty story. Tell your beautiful flowing ethereal story. Hold your story for its POWER. Hold your story. There is no story like your story EVER. Ever ever ever ever EVer – no story like your story.

Tell.

Your.

Story.

Untitled

What's your 16?
How cool is your metadata?
Have we lost our stories?
If not, where have they gone?

Hope for humanity
Wrapped up in versions
Have we lost our stories?
If not, where have they gone?

I see city streets and technotrash
Wastelands and waylaid places
Have we lost our stories?
If not, where have they gone?

The zombie apocalypse
The robotic recognition
Have we lost our stories?
If not, where have they gone?

This is not a prophecy
Only a warning
Watch out or we'll lose our stories
And then, what will we do?

Hindrances

I had a plan this morning to create a sparkly - my morning cup of
coffee, resplendent in its shiny-girly-glitteriness.
But the plans fell through and there wasn't much I could do.
So many things are this way.
Like life.
So I had to rebuild from the ashes of my failed plan.
I had to go back to square zero and regroup.
So many things are this way.
Like life.
And even though what I planned and wanted didn't happen, what art
I created made me feel *good*.
I birthed success from a derailment.
So many things are this way.
Like life.
Turn the page and be new.
Or don't.
The greatest common factor in your life is you.
So many things are this way.
Like LIFE.

Good Morning, I Don't Want to Write

I have writing to complete
I really do
My character has been nagging me
Saying "we don't hang out
Like we used to"
She says, "You're avoiding me"
I have
"You've *been* avoiding me"
I have
"Forgetting to set time for me"
There were good reasons
Life for one
She says, "my buttbone is *still* on fire"
Because that is the last scene I completed
And she is still sitting there
She would very much like to
Fight
Or pass out
Or stand up
Or *something*
Anything to move forward
She is insistent
Almost rude
"Write me out of here!"
She says
"Let me breathe!"
She says
"Only you can save me!"
She says
But I don't want to write
I don't
I'm busy
I'm sleepy
I'm out of my rhythm
And secretly
I don't want to let her go
I don't want to share her
I don't want her to go to school

Where I can't protect her
From the others
"Please"
She says
"I'm dying of boredom and Yna needs to go down!"
She cajoles
I laugh
I acquiesce
I sigh
Ok I say
I'll write today
But I'm not so sure about tomorrow
"Today is all there is, so good morning"
She says
"And you can reward yourself after
A paragraph
A page
Feel smug
Secretly accomplished
Only
Please write!"
She says
And I know
I will write today
Despite the fact
that
I don't want to

Corporate Hierarchy Poetry for the VP
From the Executive Assistant

On the other side of the wall is me
Not in look
Not in carriage
But in music, like wind, and water and joy

On the other side of the wall is you
Not in status
Not in presentation
But in drive, like a train, and steel and stabs

On the other side of the wall is us
But on this side is separation
Because you don't want to know this truth
That I am on that side of the wall with you
And you are on this side too
Closer than air but can't breathe through

On the other side of the wall is me
Womanly wiles
Feminine ways
Diva, Faerie, Heart and hand

On the other side of the wall is you
Macho macho
A real man
Dude, Homie, Logic and strength

On the other side of the wall is us
But on this side is separation
Because I don't want to know this truth
That I am on that side of the wall with you
And you are on this side too
Closer than air but can't breathe through

Don't misunderstand
I don't want to be you
Don't misread

I don't want you to be me
I only want you to respect your location
Before the train leaves the station

Because
On both sides of the wall is us
On both sides, this separation
Because we daily walk in this truth
That the wall must be
Certain like infinity
And we don't jump
And we don't move
Not because we can't
But because we don't want to

Breathing

Inhale
listening to birdsong
gentle breezes
even with engines humming underneath
Exhale
my input into the day
prayers and song
even clothed in a 6am sheath
Inhale
the smell of my garden
the taste of my coffee
the pressure on my shins from blankets or air
Exhale
my gratitude to God
my appreciation
the inspiration of stillness, just being there

I Wonder About My Fairy Folk

I wonder about my people
Where did all my Black American Fairy Folk go?
No really
Where are all the Black American Fae folk?
Did they run away
From the bad publicity
of their beauty
from the limelight
Afraid their wings would get tagged
By cultural icons
And missing status symbols
Are they on the road
Looking for role models
Moving invisibly along
Floating on their still-working
Weak and working
Battle ready and battle worn
Wings
As I drive by

I wonder about my people
Where are all the Black American fae?
born in the city
born in the snow
praising God Almighty
through their Motown
slow dancin'
with the Holy Spirit
Where did they
my people
My fae
My Black American wonders
My fae folk
go?
Surely it is a devil's trick
for me to think

I am the only
Black American fae folk
left
and I am looking for home
A home that has gone away

I wonder about my people
Is it ok
To wonder if Jesus was fae
Not FAE
But my kind
ethereal
in this world
but not of it
otherworldly magic
Can I be His kind of fae
And mix my
Good ol' Southern
Almost Baptist love
With this fae of non-worldly description
or understanding
Where did all my Black American fae folk
go?

I wonder about my people
If someone would only stand up and say
here I am
Maybe me
I'll let them see me this way
Somebody's gotta start the revival
My Black American Fae
Will you join in
or shy away
I pray you'll stand up too
And call out
sing out
cry out

stand out
just so I know you are still here
And we can praise God together
Good and loud
in tune and out of tune with our hands raised
And our wings in the air

4/5/99

Just as beautiful as LOVE
Just as hideous as PAIN
My Spirit

Power unbridled
Weakness unrestrained
My Soul

Inside the little box
Lies a world too large for discovery
My hopes

Trusted by no one
Known by all
My dreams

Easy to accept yet
Difficult to comprehend
My future

I must follow
And yet I lead
My destiny

His plan, my fate
My story
His glory

The House, The House, The House
Dedicated to Brother Mike and Church in Ramona

I have learned that

I cannot give what I do not have.

I have learned that I cannot change a single person.

I can change myself, then my home, then my environment.

A house, in a house, a part of a house,
And as the hierarchy is strengthened within me,
I thank God for the peace it has bought me.

House 1 is me, my spirit, soul and body. It is my first and deepest
root to God and to humanity.

House 2 is my family, by blood or adoption. These people should
receive the best of my time and attention from the best place just
outside of myself.

House 3 is my community, my fellow man. It is my duty to bring
whatever joy I can to these people, by involvement or absence.

~~~   ~~~   ~~~

Inside of me
Inside my house
A part of my kingdom
I am a person
Inside a group
A part of a people
I have a temple
My family is a temple
Within the kingdom known as "world"
But first my temple
And then my family
Before the world to show the world

How Much?

How much for one rib?
Bone of my bone
Flesh in my flesh
Heart and promise woven in a tapestry

How much for one rib?
Covenant spoken
Binding and bound
Life and living with peace and majesty

How much?
When the peace is tested.
How much?
When the battles come.
How much?
When the wounds try to fester.
How much?
On the long walk home?

© Tiffany Monique

When the Spirit Moves

Ok Holy Spirit
You've got three songs and some dark-room shout-outs
To arrive and prepare us to hear the message
But I just can't seem to find You in that room

Song one is fast - Watch for the ones not clapping hands
Song two is powerful - So moving the congregation's hands better
raise
Maybe I'm just too carnal
But I just couldn't find You in that room

Song three rolls right in on a practiced key change
Ok Holy Spirit - 3, 2, 1, go!
Everyone else seems to see You just fine
Move around the room

Make the same several people call out Your Holy
Messages dropped into their throats
I did what they said
Only I couldn't seem to find You in that room

I raised my hands
I sang my heart out
I even joined the choir
I couldn't find a drop of You in that room

Ok Holy Spirit
Maybe it's just me - I'm not holy enough
Didn't do enough in the allotted time
I couldn't find You in that room

Or I didn't do it at home long enough
Maybe they were right and I didn't prepare
Maybe I am just not holy at all
I couldn't find you in that room

Can I Sit Here?

I pissed the A-list off
Dagger stares and public shaming
They mocked the way I worshipped
In this little circle

I sought the advice of the ladies circle
How can I stay out of trouble here
By dressing, sitting, and serving like you
In this little circle

My skirt was always too short
My manners not proper enough
But my family name was prominent
In this little circle

I offered my services
Such as they were
They mocked me duplicitously
In this little circle

This is my forgiveness
Given and received
I never wanted that circle
And I guess it didn't want me

I Am Sorry

I apologize
To the church I left
I left
I am sorry
I learned so much
Swallowed so much
I was a good little girl
Until I vomited you out
I am so sorry
I was no martyr
I didn't save them
The ones who didn't want to leave
I didn't run rebel
Back into the building
I am sorry
I am still sad
Because so much of it was right
So much of it was beautiful
I long for the belonging of it
And I am sorry
I owe you so many apologies
For running away
To three blocks down the street
Where I had to trust God
And not the man behind the pulpit
I apologize
I AM sorry
For you
I never bowed to you
I never capitalized your calling
I would not worship you
I worship HIM
Is that my crime?
Is that why I feel guilt
I am sorry
And I still wonder
Do you point fingers
Mocking my cult attendance

Or tally my taxable tithing
Or judge my outfit
Or my worship customs
Or my mistakes
The ones you hear about passively
When I share
With those still connected to you
I am sorry
That I'm still scared
Of your judgement
That you'll say
That's what you get
With your second-hand leader
I am sorry
For the taste of you
Still in my mouth
Daring me to face you
To call your name out loud
But saying in love
That it's not too late to change
To turn around
Hard as it may be
To go back to the first Love
Not the unholy trinity
Of me, myself and I
My car, my children, my blessings
My ministry
Some say it is a bus
And I jumped off
Ages ago
But I am sorry that I am NOT sorry
I left
And I am sorry
That I am so happy to be gone
I am sorry

See

I read you like a good book
You read me like a newspaper
I see you like a beautiful text
You see me like magazine ads
I see you see I see you see
Do you see
Do you see me
Seeing you
Do you see you
See
I don't see how you can read
Knowing the intelligence of this reader
Unafraid to divulge
But verbiage is
Semantic
Do you see
I see
I see you
I see and I see
Oh, I see
See?

Just

Just this
Just this skin
aching from the inside to be scales
"gills and tails"
or something more magical than normal

Just words
Just songs and words
a conversation of pseudo-greatness
learning to lean
from my strong belief that we could grow art

And so
And so now
wings unfurling from the cocoon
repaying double
the joys stolen from an inauthentic life

~~~   ~~~   ~~~   ~~~

Who do I owe an apology to?
For pretending my voice had a limit
For stopping the flow due to fear
For ending before I began 'it'
It being me being here

What is the Shape of Your Body?
Asked by Bhanu Kapil-Rider in The Vertical Interrogation of
Strangers

It's part of American culture
Hips
Skin
A nose
Teeth
those shoes
so last season
do you have the new
is it shiny enough
is it new enough
will it get the spotlight
I AM NOT AN IT
I am not just breasts
I have them
I am not just a face
or a haircut
Can your camera zoom someone's smell
Can you mass visualize a tasty kiss
Is this all I am
All you are
Are you just hands
Can you be beautiful w/ cellulite
and acne
and dandruff
and unwanted hair
who said it was unwanted
You
Me
them
those daggone theys
Don't blame FOX
you can choose to follow
choose to beat yourself up
for not being a 5'10" 125 androgen
an alien
built of spare parts

we bought on QVC
as seen on TV
we're just full of this crap
pieces
parts
chunks
I wanna be new
whole
ME

The Whole You Naked

More than skin and blood – I am naked
More than muscle and sinew – naked
The me of me joining within the you of me
The other me barefoot in the grass
Whole, holy
Whole, wholly
When I introduce my sweet-scented self to
Tree and bush, and gypsy wagon
Everwanderer
A seed uncovered and ready to be planted
In the breeze and in the wind
Selfishly giving you to me
Not in piece and part
But complete like a fully bloomed graft
Cut out & cutting in
Telling everything by saying nothing
Because you already know
Balance by expressive truth
The blood of me hiding nowhere because it is everywhere
Revealed as wind; breeze is my bone
Inhalation is the sinew of my spirit
Ahh – I sigh completeness
Nothing to hide from & no fear of being uncovered
Because I am fully exposed
Evoking passion, peace, lunar magnetism
And the love that loves with open hands
There is a word for complete that I cannot say
But you see it like the way I am as I come toward you
Exposed soul
And glad of the voice I just realized
Was always already there
Ahh

About My Nipples

I'd like to write about my nipples. My big brown, chocolate seriously looks like Hershey's Kisses nipples. I love my nipples. They are bold, and don't like bras, and will pop out to say hello, no matter how much padding I have over them, but I like how resilient they are.

I think of slavery and I think of babies, and I think of sex and I think of pleasure, and I think of God. My nipples serve God. Imagine (*Ee mah hee nay*).

The taste of them is something I know intrinsically, though not from experiencing them the way others have. How exotic and cinnamon they are.

My doctor tried to tell me there was cancer behind them, but it turned out to be nothing. My nipples celebrated all day. I am so involved with my pectoral lighthouses.

Once a month they seethe with need to grow milk for a child that I am not having nine months from the moment they sense awareness. For about a week they are sad, and perhaps a bit petulant. Sensitive they are. Oh yes. On so many levels.

I want to marry them to my husband's body. I want to feed them to my children. I want them fertile with milk, and passion, and love, and sensation, and hope, and joy, and rest, and satiation.

I also want them to not stick out so I can wear silk shirts sometimes!

My Violin of an Armpit

My violin of an armpit
I play across it sometimes
With the bow of a razor blade
Or sometimes
Pizzicato tickles from the fingertips of my love
Or the warm water of my shower
My violin of an armpit
Carnal are my curves
When I turn my head just right
Chinrest becomes my shoulder
I play the body of my body
Preludes via prescreens
Stinger strikes of pain
Scars like harmonics
The string of my soul
The orchestra of my aroma
Shifting and turning like movements
A symphony

~~~ ~~~ ~~~

A Letter

I missed you hamstring.
Inner thigh tried to come between us.
We used to hang out with knees and calves at the beach, and in our dresses.
Old crones would call us provocative and promiscuous.
Perhaps we were.
But we are gonna hang out soon, and more.
You deserve your time in the sun.

My Thighs

Not to be arrogant or proud, but I speak without talking, and I speak loud
See the way the hips slide nice, well, that ain't all that should make you look twice
Sex appeal- got it.
Front and back too
But you don't have my eyes or point of view
And if that's all you want, I gotta move

My thighs are beautiful and strong, but that's NOT all that I have going on
My mouth is sensual and my tongue is strong, but I use it for conversation
Know what I can do
And do it well
But my sex is no longer for sale
I seek to celebrate all that makes me female

I have the skills and desire to please, but there is so much more to me
You wanna piece of me, dripping and sweet, but I am a meal- not a taste of meat
I'll no longer settle
I know I can wait
Because I want the soul to resound in my mate
And for him alone, my thighs were made to satiate
My things, my rise, my mouth, my crown
To God and then him will I happily bow down

Joints

My joints are not separated
All these parts are all me
Like a body jazz influences
Roots to a multi-facet-tree
And I am a heart
And I am a song
And I am a lover
And my ride is long

This journey was hard on my joints you see
I have been greatly wrong and profoundly right
I see things like music
And wasted time is kryptonite
Still I am a heart
Still I am a song
Still I am a lover
Still my ride is long

But then I have to ask myself
Is time in the cocoon truly wasted?
For all the pushing through to flight
For all blood from grinding teeth tasted
Because I am a heart
Because I am a song
Because I am a lover
Because my ride is long

Feeling vibrant like the water
Roots that will go nowhere
Flowing gifts like a fountain
From this my heart
From this my song
From this my loving
From this my riding long

Bend and stretch me I won't break
My joints are stronger than my perception
As long as I live I'll I give you what I can
Blessed in my giving and your reception
Through this my heart
Through this my song
Through this my love
Through my journeying on

Cycle

I am not sure what is happening
Could I be giving birth or something?
Or maybe I am just awakening myself
Awakening *to* myself?
The sleeping dragon everyone seems to see
But me
I am this
I love this
This *me*
But I am only barely aware of how to
Be this me
Even as I am experiencing the being
Of this me
This strong
This powerful
This dragon
This queen feminine
This woman
In me
In other women
In little girls
I see dragon seeds in us all
Some sleeping
Some unborn
Some stillborn
My seedling is shining in spite of my self-understanding
Contraction
Upon contraction
Awakening
Level by level
Dream by dream
Muscle
Bone
Fire
Stone
Heart
I have been giving birth to me my whole life
I suppose I will never stop until I die

The Art of Shutting Up

You can only have attention
if you take it
if you are quiet
then you are nothing
if however
you are good at limelight
then you are too loud
and you should be ashamed
or obnoxious
I guess
I don't have the art of shutting up
I don't have a face
I am only a mouth
only
you don't hear this
word
me
you say shut
up
I can't
just
be
you make me feed
for life
like I am an animal
and you own me
well
screw it
you won't listen
anyway
may as well
enjoy myself
making
you
as
UN
comfortable
as you make

me
shutting up
is an art
I don't have
I gave it away
so I could breathe
even though
I love you
and am only trying to
ju
s
t
be
with you
ju
s
t
be
with you
ju
s
t
be
all sides
of
me

Our Cocoons

Our cocoons are
Opening up
Lots of things
Gifts
Losses
Changes
Like wings unfurling
Strengthened through pressure
Slow cracks
Bits of light and air
Filtering through mucus
Change is wet sometimes
Sticky
Smells funny
Unpretty
Not always for public consumption
Despite being in public view
My scars are
Where the magic is
My joy
Hidden in
Absolutely nothing
Healings
Amputations
Imperfections
Like kisses
"I love your scars baby"
Maturity is
Delicious
Opening up
Breaking
Down
Through
Up
Over
Breathing it in and out
And in and out
Like music

See this now
My own and yours
Ours
Hearts
Beat and blood
Blood and bone
Bone and wing
Wing and sky
Our cocoons are
Opening up

Dreams and Maelstroms

I am a poem
rewriting and rewritten
I am a fortress coming down
coming out
I am a green heart
being pruned
The work is hard
and rewarding
But it's never been about me
has it?
God's timing is perfect
and hilarious

~~~ ~~~ ~~~ ~~~

There's a coldness welling up inside me. It's in the back, rather
quieted, but sneaking like Gollum. Sneaking. Like smoky splinters
up my spine.
I remember staring at this shadow before.
I danced as it waited, side to side
a bobbing shadow.
I see thinly veiled cruelty at all the hope in place.
The coldness hates the hope.
The coldness is highly annoyed by hope's shiny brightness,
at her warm effervescence.
The coldness is sneaking,
trying to catch hope unawares.
The problem is that hope shines so bright that the coldness can't
jump out from behind any shadows.

Opaque Glass Houses

People in glass houses don't throw stones
To be left with the shards when they're all alone
I wasn't some object frail and weak
Too hurt and blind to be able to speak

But he played his game...

Give me a reason to say it's all right
When I'm not even sure I've survived the night
I heard his movements, shuffling as he parted
I don't want to play this game that he's started

He made me...

Comfort me though you don't know how
I'm lost in a labyrinth I can't figure out
That unexpected touch will be my demise
Hidden in the corner, the secret in his eyes

I'm holding on for dear life...

Don't say healing is there because I don't see it
Don't tell me I'll be fine- I'll never believe it
Opaque glass houses will be my shrines
Life has a rhythm, and I'm lost in a rhyme

What if I just let go?

Bloodlust

You would think...
Me terrified
It is time now
The birthing
This truth
This ugly, angry, truth
Eviscerating me from the inside
The battle of pride, and rage, and carnage, and vengeance
But I like it
The power of the fight within to get out
Taking me over

You would think...
Me unaccepting of my death
This internal immolation as I birth the stillborn lies I've carried
Only the husk will remain
The husk of the seed
The seed that had to die
So that the warrior could be harvested

You would think...
It must be dark magic
But it is most HOLY
This truth is coming
This fighter is awakening
Come on!

You would think...
Me unexcited in the throes of such agony
Me expecting acutely spent when the birthing is done
But I'm itching for battle now
And I will be
Reborn fighting
I dare you to underestimate me

You would think...

Impact Tremors

Not just the immediate metamorphosis
Not just the first seven layers of shifting skin
Something more is happening
Fathoms down
It's just too deep to see right now
But the water in the glass is moving
As it sits idle on the table
And I know it to be true
Something deep is moving
The smell of the air is affected
Flying things have shifted their patterns
Burrowing things have begun to move
Some rising to the surface
Others relocating
Where they are going, I don't know
It's just too deep to see right now
The occasional pebble does a gentle dance
Portents of the coming calamity
Or perhaps triumphant return of a deep truth
The crystallization within the geode
As it is beginning to break open
To shine forth
But I can't see it
Only I know it to be true
It's just too deep to see right now
But the certainty of it
Is humming low in the throat
In the chest
In the gut
In the crotch
In the knees
In the undersides of the feet
It's just too deep to see right now

Can You Guess?

A closed window book.
A pursed lip with stern condescension.
It's Parisian smoky black & white mornings with cold damp war
wounds and nearly silent rain.
It's a most sad song that catches in your throat.
The unselfish death of a dreamed life somewhere far away in your
own back yard.
This...sanity.
This question.
This naked form not quite 17 and still apologizing for being
someone's unrequited dreamscape.
A long walk still not taken.
A joke still untold.
An unchewed gum of a thing.
A masterpiece not started, and I just realized what I'm describing.

Exquisite

Tickle me sweetly
No gray clouds here
When the smile comes
a shining
Wish me a-secret
No regrets here
When the love comes
a healing
Kiss me most truly
No truth shamed here
When the time comes
I'm ready

~~~ ~~~ ~~~

And just like that
Words come from a stranger
and I quote
"Exquisite sacred pleasure
Exquisite sacred pain
Pregnant silence"
And I am once again reminded
Write
The beautiful music of poetry
Write
The stories untold
Write
The perspectives of the forgotten
I won't apologize for the rest of my life
I was right there
I was writing there
And just like that
Words from a stranger

Considering a Paradox

All those days
All those times
All these days
All these times
Past passes in the present
into future
And I am me, here
in this timeless place
Wondering what time it is
wishing at a wishing well not made
yet already ruined
and standing beautifully in the garden
Statues know my name
And countless blades of grass
like heartbeats, so important
despite being so easily overlooked
So powerful, yet come and gone so quickly
All those days
All these days
And I am here
Wondering what time it is

Theme & Variations

I've heard it said
A great many things about
Dynamic duos
Complimentary opposites
The dance and not the battle
Heard that last week
In and out
Red and blue
Blue and grey
Yin and yang
Yanantin and masintin
Partners in a samba
Can they dance alone?
Can I?
On the dancefloor called corpus callosum
The moonlight and shadow
One orb
The storyteller and the administrative assistant
Breathing
Both directions are necessary
For life
Body
Hands feet
Left side right side
Seen unseen
Wolf wife
That's for Clarissa
Who started this whole conversation
Without even knowing I existed
Or perhaps
It was Tannen
She said it is communication
That can destruct meaning
Goffman's impressions
Given and given off
Gilligan's pleasure
Relationship for relationships
And all the stories in between

And around
And throughout
Can they dance alone?
Can I?
Thanks Anne
For your friend Kitty
Imaginary and real
Realized
Shange's choreo-poem
Embodiment?
The dance of communication
Or beauty
Or therapy
A mushroom, Alice
Eat it
One side makes you bigger
And the other...
Otherizing
Let's bring in Pme and Qme
Honne and Tatamae
There I am
In the conversation
Of duality
Recognizing and engaging
Via dual-expression
Write it
Then say it
No
Say it
THEN write it
One feeds the other better in this way
This way that way
Light shadow
Felt sense felt senses
Hearing with ears
Our words
Our woman-self words
Can they dance alone?
Can I?
Front self Pme

Meta-self Qme
Winding a winding road
To knowing
To gnowing
Knowing and gnowing
Oracle and Architect
Archetypes
Popular culture
Myth story
Can they dance alone?
Can I?

To Busboys and Poets

"A bird can love a fish"
But where would they live?
In the heart
Or the belly
Of a dog
He holds her there
She holds him
His gun
The gun
Giving life...
Taking life...
Shooting pink hearts
Out of a green gun
And she is on her knees
With her back to me
Clear and not quite here
The image is devoid of explanation
And almost too of color
Lines as kissing cousins
Warp and weft
Weaving and winding
Creating images
Truths
Lies
Isn't that the game?
To be the bird
To love the fish
In the belly of a dog
In the bullet of a gun
Let one line bind
And then unbind

~~~   ~~~   ~~~   ~~~

Love can complete
The incomplete thought
And from the place
From the drawing of the line

From the painter
From the mind
Deep within the beautiful mind
Love can live
This many-leveled
Picture

One Dream in Prose

I dreamed of a man
He was selling wares
(the only one at market)
Everyone bought pieces that were shiny
I chose fabric
I didn't know when I chose it
but that fabric
matched the man's
He and I wore dark crimson
And I was trying to save a boy
a little boy
He fell against the wall
or perhaps he was thrown
The man calmed me
saying the boy was in no more danger
Then we regarded each other
He saw what I wore
or perhaps
he just acknowledged
that I matched him
We knew what we were to each other
A performer stood behind us
in purple
I did not trust her
because she'd chosen a shiny cloth
She was jealous
of the man and I
matching
but she had chosen
her fabric
on her own

I See Dying People

I am surrounded by children these days
There are so many hiding in nakedness
Crying out in disrespectful retorts
Begging to be seen for who they truly are & loved in spite of
themselves
They scream laughter because they don't know how much they hurt
They don't want to know
They are afraid to look at their own brokenness
See how scared they are
Of being left behind and looked over
I see them like scenes in a horror film
Long drawn faces of despair
Beggars in a marketplace
Covered in dirty lies and smeared makeup
Scars of lost time and lost hope
They are dying, shouting as they suffocate
Can I come up for air?
Don't leave me behind!
See me! Save me! Love me!
I am surrounded by the beautiful young
Free in body while bound in mind
I am surrounded by their absent looks
And their rage against hopelessness
Tears behind rolled eyes
Afraid to speak, because they have so much to say

I Was Considering

Death is dead
But everybody dies
It is appointed to them
An inevitable gift
A beautifully known surprise

Death is dead
But everybody dies
I am not afraid of it
But I am not sure of it
It is the unknowing I despise

Death is dead
But everybody dies
Curiosity killed the cat
Satisfaction brought it back
But the dead do not rise
The season is changing
The tide turning
But the dead do not rise

The road less taken
Is still taken
But the dead do not rise

Armies rage and conquer
Political
But the dead do not rise

Lovers come together
Love is lost
But the dead do not rise

Harbinger

This pain you bring
Succinct
Acute
Accurate to the tale about to be told
Beautiful pain
Resulting in exquisite promise
The story
Once stone
Breaking forth
You bring anticipation of coming things
Change
Through struggle
Through changing
You are the beacon
Each travail a cavalry charge
The harvest birthing
Destiny preparing
Its name called out
By you

dry souls

dry souls smell like dead dreams sometimes
raisins, yes, shrivelled by time
scratchy when they pass you by
jealous of your wings

dry souls hunt for your living blood
but lack the energy to do any good
they just smell of rotted fruit
curious people things

dry souls sing with fetid mouths
moments, seconds, minutes, hours
they lie constantly of their powers
chanting hateful songs

dry souls lay in wait for weakness
misrepresenting those born to meekness
within a facade they claim eliteness
hiding plagues and seeds gone wrong

dry souls have claws in their commentary
vilifying those lives not sedentary
defining disease as those not ordinary
"normal" is *their* land

dry souls waste away parasitically
living off the living just to die inevitably
still they clamour with whispering
chorus of the damned

"Yes dry souls do all of those things but why do they do those things?" -Sarah Dickerson

Fear I think, moves the beauty from a journey
Making it desolate
a dry soul wanders in the desolate plains
of cynicism and hurt and perhaps fear of being hurt again

Hurt I think, disables the soul from proper travel
Making it root
a dry soul unable to move to the waters of life
of forgiveness, of true rest, a perhaps hope of engaging joy

I was a dry soul once, afraid and hurt
Why did I do the things I did then?
Thank God someone brought me water
told me to forgive them and then
the harder work of forgive myself
releasing in the loving, painful pushes
every blood-lined wrinkle

And for my pain and work
my soul is not dead
my soul is not dry
I take every pain and joy with all their weight
and remember my dry days
so that I never - even when living in a desert
live the death that is life as a dry soul

Sometimes

Sometimes you are the paper
Sometimes you are the sand
Sometimes you're being prepared
Sometimes it's where you land

Sometimes it ain't just sometimes
And you're a little stuck
Metamorphose butterfly
Or be a moth - if you want

You're gonna grow on anyway
You're gonna go from here
Time don't stop for no one
Not even you my dear

Sometimes you're in the desert
Sometimes you're in the sea
Sometimes you are flying
Busy little bee

You can go to the South Pole
And touch it on the tip
So you can say the world revolved around you
For just a little bit

But mostly you can forgive yourself
Give up being in control
Sometimes you have to bow your head
Admit you're wrong and let go

Sometimes you are the paper
Sometimes you are the sand
Sometimes you're being prepared
Sometimes it's where you land

In the Desert - part 1
Dedicated to Seddy Bear & my daughters

I am happily
In the desert
In the dry season
Preparing
I get to be here, waiting for You
This little mouse, I
This lioness, I
I question
Is it better
To be a smart mouse
Or
A dumb lioness
Or
Both
One quiet, unassuming
Often overlooked
One a natural predator
Often fought for her alpha role
I am in the desert, waiting for You
Both mouse and lioness
Learning to be both
Learning to be neither
I am happily
In the desert
In the dry season
Waiting for You

~~~   ~~~   ~~~

In the Desert - part 2
It's flippin' dry!
I'm parched!
Need fluids!
Need to LIVE!
Well,
If I'm alive enough to complain
I'm ALIVE!

HECK NO
it's not comfortable!
But there's something beautiful in it
Beauty in the pain of change
A strength stirring as I learn
I am in fact *not* dry
Or parched
Or in need of anything
As if I lay dying
Because all I've done
Is left my comfort zone
And I have to say...
I'm kinda diggin' the difference
Kinda

Apologies 4 not 1

I danced near a desert sea
Top down in a Camero
Whooshing through the
Desert of Goodbye
There was joy in this
My departure from the
Desert
And apologies for not one
Moment of my stay there

I walked away from a cycle
A life of no winged travel
Taking root in
Perpetual past review
I am free to go
Not just on parole
Free
And apologies for not one
Moment of my education

~~~ ~~~ ~~~

I have no inclinations
To resume past limitations But I thank you for the trip And
apologies for not one Moment of my life lived thus far

Mirrors I

I've seen some awesome things in rear view mirrors
And I've captured my share of crystalline moments
They are snapshots
That will never come again

I glorified what was behind me
Going full speed toward tomorrow
I claimed those minuscule times and places
Captured like prisoners of war

I tried to warn myself
And now I think I'm *finally* listening to my own advice
Looking back is awesome
Staring back is deadly

I must remember
Mirrors show beautiful reflections
Even though what is in them
Are immortalized battles and brutalities

Along with timeless joys and beauties
Mirrors are amulets
A most powerful force
Not to be taken lightly

Untitled

He moves so fast
the air blurs
and time has to chase him
That's how my mouth is
Gotta slow down
Let what I say have the momentum
Of reality
Immaturity screams by
at breakneck speed
And the clean-up is
too much for even FEMA
Let what I say have the insulation
Of adulthood
He moves so fast
his arms become ribbons
That's how my anxiety can be
Gotta be calm
Let how I respond be grounded
Deeply rooted
Wind-driven waves of circumstance
Can overturn fossilized sequoia forests
Let how I respond be noble
Almost royal
He moves so fast
That's how I can be
The art of being still
Starts with admitting turbulence
The art of growing up
Starts with admitting childishness
He moves as a child
My soul is like a child
They both will grow
Despite themselves

On Display

I can not hide my quirks
I've tried it & it don't work
I am not an introvert
But I may as well be
On some days
I am so strong I set my cracks
On display
I am sometimes a hypocrite
And all I can do is look at it
But
But
But
I am still here
And I am not done
Getting better
So let's take a look at me
Or let's take a look at you and see
Who the most jacked up will be
FBI or CIA
May find the funky laundry in which
our closeted skeletons play
I can no more judge you
Than I can rob a bank or two
But
But
But
We are still here
And we are not done
Getting better

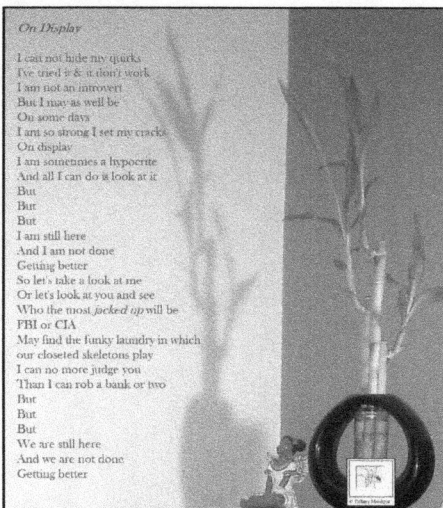

Stain on My Shirt

I'm full of little mistakes
Idiosyncrasies, small breaks
Like tiny holes in my pants
And marks on my skin

See I'm alive with bruised magic
Almost great, yet almost pathetic
Dingy white, small wrinkles
Legs to muscular, on ankles too thin

There are a lot of glitches
The little girl, in life's large britches
I'll always almost be fine
But on a small technicality I'm hurt

Somehow I travel through life
As normal as a man loving his ex-wife
The weirder you are, the cooler you'll be
By my differences are subtle-

~ Like a stain on my shirt

Windows

The limits of my future are like dusty windows
The view of my soul while
My spirit waits
Feeling as profitable as unused gas,
Psyche encased in a boring rhythm
Lather, rinse, repeat
Looking in the rear view mirrors
Lather, rinse, repeat
My soul
Lather
Rinse
Repeat
Can I get off this train
I mean, the view back there is beautiful and all
But I got places to go
My body like a car
My mind like a map
My spirit like a call
Take me where I wanna go
Forward

Private Path, Locked Door

He moves so fast
the air blurs
and time has to chase him
That's how my mouth is
Gotta slow down
Let what I say have the momentum
Of reality
Immaturity screams by
at breakneck speed
And the clean-up is
too much for even FEMA
Let what I say have the insulation
Of adulthood
He moves so fast
his arms become ribbons
That's how my anxiety can be
Gotta be calm
Let how I respond be grounded
Deeply rooted
Wind-driven waves of circumstance
Can overturn fossilized sequoia forests
Let how I respond be noble
Almost royal
He moves so fast
That's how I can be
The art of being still
Starts with admitting turbulence
The art of growing up
Starts with admitting childishness
He moves as a child
My soul is like a child
They both will grow
Despite themselves

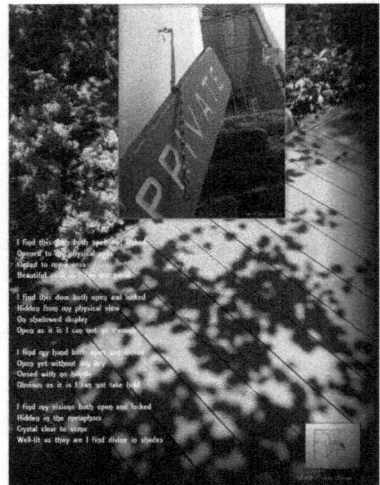

Mirrors II

He moves so fast
the air blurs
and time has to chase him
That's how my mouth is
Gotta slow down
Let what I say have the momentum
Of reality
Immaturity screams by
at breakneck speed
And the clean-up is
too much for even FEMA
Let what I say have the insulation
Of adulthood
He moves so fast
his arms become ribbons
That's how my anxiety can be
Gotta be calm
Let how I respond be grounded
Deeply rooted
Wind-driven waves of circumstance
Can overturn fossilized sequoia forests
Let how I respond be noble
Almost royal
He moves so fast
That's how I can be
The art of being still
Starts with admitting turbulence
The art of growing up
Starts with admitting childishness
He moves as a child
My soul is like a child
They both will grow
Despite themselves

Thoughts on

Looked back at milestones
Realized late bloomer flight
Walked back into the room of my life
And saw it was quite bright

Thought it wasn't good enough
Thought it simply wouldn't do
Listened to the them's and they's
Lived life so that they'd approve

But then

Regarded the army again
Realized it was small but tight
Walked around my armory
My battlements still ready to fight

Changed my thinking over time
Bloomed beautiful and true
See a different future now
So many more things I want to do

Coffee Colored Word Play

Eating the delicious steam of poetry
Embracing coffee
My mind is a concrete web of eternity blowing peace inside a
breeze to wear
this daughter
not ferocious, not porcelain, not color, wet like a fish though
seeping here
telling myself, "know their yesterday"
as I sip to sips of wind
of air
and listening always to my own sacred rhythm
that I can't spell
but I hide it in the coffee of my color
like the crème in my own nutty flavor
seeping, steeping
wafting through the web that is perhaps NOT so concrete
learning to trust in the ferocious
learning to bellow
breeze and wind
the effect is not the cause
knowing their yesterday assists my eternity, my poetry
my daughter
delicious wet steam, streaming
air & breathing
I desire to be pierced by a thousand sacred rhythms
pick two, making one, mine, here, now
and breathe it, embrace it
let it make me wet – like a fish, like eternity, like peace
mutually exclusive and ever interwoven
and relevant, and ferocious
so many more to come
I am pregnant with my coffee colored daughter destiny

Note to the Fallen

You are not allowed to give up on yourself
You are simply NOT allowed
She needs you
He needs you
They need you
I need you
There is nothing wrong with hurting
Pruning is not meant to be comfortable
Learning not to live by thorn
But by rose
Living outside the walls
Of your own comfort zone
You are not allowed to give up on yourself
NOT allowed
Here at the end of this journey
Just before your own coronation
Not of your entire journey
But of this moment
There are other adventures to be had
Far beyond this one
Far far beyond
You are not allowed to give up on yourself
You are NOT allowed to give up
The world needs you

On Self-amputation

Forgiveness is an Amputation
Self-amputate if necessary
Cry
Write
Cry
Cry
Write
Cry
Then smile
Because you remember
Then cry some more
Healthy plants get pruned
THAT CRAP HURTS!
But then you look
And see it is growing back
Sinews and tendons can
And do
Grow back
Some choices hurt
Some only seem to

~~~   ~~~   ~~~   ~~~

Inspired by the Phrase I
"I like to tell that story because it makes me look smart. There are other stories I don't like to tell...Pain is the teacher you never forget." -Roy H Williams

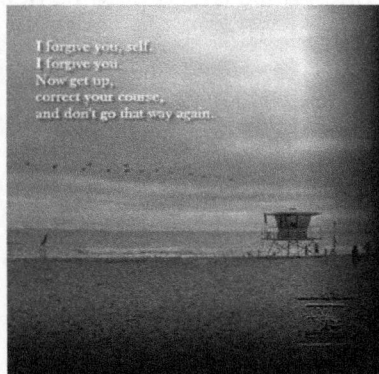

I forgive you, self.
I forgive you.
Now get up,
correct your course,
and don't go that way again.

Inspired by the Phrase II
"Danger is very real, but fear is a choice." -Will Smith, After Earth

I will say it
I will give no quarter to the lie
The bind
The one that says I must say less
Give less
Be less
Because it scares you
(and by the way, if you ain't "you", then don't take ownership)
I will give it
I will open my heart to the sunshine
The freedom
The joy
Even in a moment
(and by the way, if you've been there with me, cool)
I will feel it
I will wear the full armour
Not apologizing
Not compromising
Accepting everything that I am to you, with you, for you
(All the many "you's" out there)
I will choose
Choose life
Choose faith
Choose me
Choose the promise
I will be the fearless one I once tried not to be because of you
(Though I thank you for the trip)
I will change
I am a shifting rhythm
In the poem of life
In the life of a poem
And I am not written by you
(Though I have been edited by "you" from time to time)

Inspired by the Phrase III
You're just a product of some negative thinking...just a little self-confidence and coordination and you're gonna be fine" - Diana Ross, The Wiz

When MJ sang out, "You caint win"
I wanted to sock him in the chin
I have never been the corporate type
Even when I worked for them in jail, I mean pinstripes
Toto bit a lion and so did I
His was a cat, mine was my pride
But I am still standing here with my fist up
Despite all the times I messed up
Pour the oil in my joints please
I'll go where my destiny points me
The one with my name on it; that's the one I want.
The pen engraved specific to my creative font
The chair that most perfectly fits
All of my cross-legged sits
The braids that warp and weft my hair
Causing ethnically weighted stares
Let me not the Wizard of Oz be
I have my own girl-child magic seed
The Wiz to the Wizard's Dorothy
Go on and slide some oil to me
I have places to be and go
I'll follow *and* build the yellow brick road

In Homage to William Shakespeare

A Sonnet on the Move

Let me join the ones to stand up like this
Takes a healing hold and a strength to be
Pressed into the truth I now try to live
No more falsehood, bluff, technicality
Couldn't truly live as afraid and false
Most eyes seem so clear. Why can they not see?
Thrill me with the past jealousies of all
I am. No longer bound to not love me
Will not lose again that much of myself
To shine like a sun lit with bitterness
Won't assign again my own heart to hell
The cost to be free is that I forgive
If hope is my call and honour my name
Let us now load cannons. Let me take aim.

In Homage to William Shakespeare

Of Anticipation

Notice of late, anticipation
Predictability's fair muse
To move in sync ahead of pulsations
And still managing to slide the groove
Grimace when you're out of step
Intending to be right on course
Glow even as your voice is left
Sold to highest bidder - popularity's whore
It is not easy on the fly
Slipping in to follow suit
Everyone uniquely alike
Despite the war and search for truth
Learn the steps and do the dance
Yet take your solos at each appropriate chance

In Homage to William Shakespeare

But Biding, I Live Beyond My Own Love

■ ■

Just so you have an idea of where this would take place in the great love story, Romeo and Juliet *by 'The Bard' himself.*

Everyone exits with his or her lessons learned, and Juliet awakes in a stupor of pain and blood loss. She grieves her husband in one last monologue before Romeo's ghost (which may or not be visible) either leads her offstage or becomes apparent to her. In that case, she falls over his body, and the lights go out, per the director.

This was a wonderful way to spend a Saturday.
■ ■

Juliet rouses half-conscious over Romeo. She is bleeding from her stab wound and in great pain.

My lover dead and nothing shall be done
And I, a widow and failed suicide;
My hour of twilight and I see no fault.
T'was love that moved me thus; and thus I move
With this my life's blood spilt, still flowing life

Juliet pulls out the dagger, and it falls on Romeo's body. She caresses his face with her bloody hand.

My budding blossom, corrupt and fading,
Or perhaps, now wakening to a truth.
I may not die here. I could live, for him.
My life's blood, poisoned with this rank knowledge
That neither life nor death will end my love,
And this pain as sweet as it is morbid.
My Romeo is no more. Oh, cruel fate!
The warp and weft of lost innocences
Cast us down from joy; laughing whilst we died.
Our marriage bed thus turned into a grave,
And yet here I lay cast back from Hades;
Rejected both by life and death am I—
To look upon the lips now cold to me

The arms with haste retreat away from me
Both sepulcher and marriage bed denied.

She takes his hand.

Let me make of him a sweet eulogy—
Him who holds my heart but now not my hand;
For Romeo. Only for Romeo.
Do I live or die or reach or rest here?
My heart betwixt my fingers slipping sand
In spite of my death. I can feel my life.
Reason with me now why the dagger sings
And why the pain hums as I bleed away;
The sentence LIFE for the fair Juliet
Even as Romeo will don his wings.
More fool I to sit here as the crone would.
No more young maiden; never mother be.
My husband in dream and reality.
On our most hidden wedding night, he came
And planted his root, but it did not seed.
And now his dagger. And again my blood
No, I cannot live. To whom do I plead?
Oh, nurse! Apothecary! Kind Friar!
My voice a whispered prayer to my own self—
Survive to lie here crying and lonely.
No charm to move me and I will not go!

Juliet tries to take the dagger but, too weak to lift it, she drops it to the ground.

My tortured treasure here with Romeo.
Ah! Pain renews me. Has my prayer been heard?
To see him shortly, I would stab again!
Had I the strength to; it would be just so.
Eviscerate myself happily, yes!

She falls over Romeo's body.

My head becomes stone, heavy it lays down
Again on his chest, cooler than before.

Would that I could slake my thirst for his lips
But weariness brings its own heavy crown.

She weakly begins running her fingers over his body.

Perhaps a touch then; blessed fingertip
Run scores of courses over his body.
Leave memories of morning lovemaking.
My husband and I consummated once
And now those trails with fingertips bloody.
My Romeo. My freedom and my death.
To question my choice to die with no thought
Of my life, before Romeo claimed me,
Before I even thought to claim myself.
I was love's fool. And for my love, I fought
And died to live and see him, die again.
My breath is short upon my breast my love.
Do meet me at the gate to then usher
The putrefaction of both our bodies;
Yours slightly before mine as I follow.
And what of now? I cleave to you my love.
I'm yours in life and death to satiate.
If I die, I die for you and still live
A promise kept; a promise still keeping.
And if I live, I swear it's not too late
In grave grotesqueries, we shall still be!
You are the king of my mortal decay
And yet, I defy somehow your mandate
To live and die at your behest my love.
Did you not do that for me? Show the way!
So that my womb will only spawn your dreams.
Your decomposing children in me grow—
I yearn to mother. Perhaps now in death
We shall rule the ghosts that shall come for us.
Our mortal coils a harvest that will show
The madness of our fated love and deaths;
A song of youthful frenzy turned to blood.

Juliet begins singing softly

Your name, a noose I tied about my neck
Refrains of a song sung in misery
Of families whose hate bred hate and love.
Oh death my dance partner, may he cut in?
I am and am not yours to command now.
My eyes see nothing, my fingertips numb—
Yes, blessed sleep with him, my Romeo.

She gasps and reaches out.

My husband is here and shall now lead me out!

Satan and a Spot
To Ed Coonce

FARCE: noun
1. A comic dramatic work using buffoonery and horseplay and typically including crude characterization and ludicrously improbable situations.

Satan complained about his bad monkey
The one Ed bought him
As a Secret Santa gag gift
A running joke from East Hell
Along with the pink beanie & ball cap
Back then at a party
(We gave the ball cap to the monkey)
I told Satan I wouldn't date him
Not anymore
He seemed nonplussed by that
And still called me for booty at oh dark thirty
I told him to go back to East Hell
And I blocked his number
Unfriended him on Facebook
Stopped following him on Twitter
That's when Shakespeare's spot showed up
It moved in with me
And didn't do much
But look forlorn
Pining for Shakespeare
Pining for poor mad Hamlet
I was almost sad about it
Then I figured, I'd rather have the spot
Than Satan and his monkey

Ed Coonce replied, "Satan has a monkey. He never asked for one. It came in the mail one day."

The Difference
Inspired by **Robert Frost**

"Two roads diverged in a wood"
And you took them both
Sometimes you want so bad to travel on a particular road
And despite the detour signs,
Construction men,
And police ribbons
You find yourself hurt that the way is impossible to travel
It'll take a minute,
Regrouping
Learning the new way
(Thank GOD for G.P.S.)
And then you turn yourself around
And you get going on the right road
Yes
You're annoyed at the time you lost
At the ground you gave up
Due to wrong turn choices
But then you see this road is much easier
And faster
And your vehicle isn't suffering
From the unnecessarily rugged twists
Turns,
Obstacles,
Roadblocks
And you get to where you were trying to go
Which was the exact place you were trying to go
When you were going the wrong way
But this new way
So much more beautiful
And easy
And you realize how lucky you are
To know the difference so thoroughly

9-10-11
For Autumn Jade

The duplicity of duplication
Her brand-new eyes
My brand-new eyes
What she sees is me
What I see is me
What she sees is new
What I see is new too
My family
My blood
So different
And the same
Her eyes
My eyes
Her perception
My reception
Autumn Jade
A beautiful jewel harvested
And a beloved harvest
A new life
And a new life
We say Happy New Year
It is
It really is a Happy New Year
For her
It really is a Happy New Year
For me

Redefining Family

What does the word Family mean to you?
When someone says, "Show me your family"
Where do you look to?

Is it a person you seek, a duo, a team?
Tell a lie, tell the truth
Live the American Dream

My fam, my clique, crew, set, posse, clan
All for one, or a smoking gun
Depends on who's in the plan

Do you cut off limbs if 'they' hurt you or yours?
If enough time passes
Will you reopen closed doors?

I admit my definition has shifted with age
I claim no full knowledge
Experience is my sage

Family meant persons for whom I'd die
When someone hurt my family
I was ready to fight

Blood was not the qualifier, and my list was *long*
Friends forever wasn't said
But when I said friend, the bond was strong

I've begun to see family with a more open hand
They must make their own choices
Their own dreams, their own stand

Sometimes they have to go out and learn they were wrong
So that the family can come together
Sing a more connected song

Perspective taints reality where family is concerned
What you see isn't what you get
A penny saved is a lesson learned

Sometimes the best gift of family is time away
If only to gain some part of
The perspective we let stray

Long losts return and we say welcome
Though their eyes seem world-wearied
And distant from home

We forget the stolen clothes and hateful words
And we remember the cracking up
Random things, like jokes on birds

And we see then through the glasses that love has us wear
We heal from the hurts
And bind up the tears

Strangely that family will not perfect
We just see them differently
As life makes us reflect

Sometimes the ritual includes the explosion
Joyous hugs at first
Then negative drama and emotion

And hurting people continue hurting, while 'ouches' still occur
But the love manages and grows
No matter how much "nicer" we wish they were

Prodigal sons, daughters, fathers and mothers too
But of course this is my opinion
What does FAMILY mean to you?

I Want to Tell Them...
For Moses

Not lost nor loss
A heart or a hand
Not a time or in time
Just a feeling
Liminal
Quickened and then
Slowed to nothing
There was and is pain
But never yours to bear
That day
Maybe you were
Waving goodbye
With your tiny tiny hand
I thought different
But now I wonder
Did your little soul know?

~~~   ~~~   ~~~

Blessed by blood and bone
Portents of a coming love
Dark days contract
A beautiful harvest of life to come
I am not my own
I never really was
And you
You were
ultimately
never mine

Things My Mama Says

Let's make a memory
If it happened more than five minutes ago
- don't bring it up
Hurt people hurt people
Aww sugar foot!
Ninaaaaa nina buttbutt
…and jelly
Michael Jackson and Janet Jackson are the same person
Keep family business in the family
God gave me a TEAM
What the ham sandwich?!
I just want you to be happy
And she keeps saying things
Every day
I don't want to forget
But I already have started
Misplacing the millions of tidbits so vital to me
Or maybe they're still germinating
Too busy bearing fruit to be quoted

Ugly Drawers, Pretty Panties

Beautifully awkward
Every joint supplies
Thumb, thigh, lip, hip
From the grave to the skies
Ugly drawers, pretty panties
That's my family

15 minutes of fame
Six to zero degrees
Elbows, spine, ears, hair
Lifted hands and bended knees
Ugly drawers, pretty panties
That's my family

I forgot I was loved
Lost it in a lie of fear
Wrist, chest, abs, calves
I've returned home and everyone is here
Ugly drawers, pretty panties
That's my family

My daughters are not lost
My sons are on their way
Ankle, knuckle, biceps, triceps
I loved you long before today
Ugly drawers, pretty panties
That's my family

Some by blood and some by blood
Adoption sacred and true
Palms, skull, thighs, eyes
I never let go of you
Ugly drawers, pretty panties
That's my family

Yes, I said it
No too many would
Heart, head, hand, land
What's mine is mine, and He made it good
Ugly drawers, pretty panties
That's my family

4c With a White Man

My nappy hair was our second date
He laughed before he tried to relate

He tried to run his fingers through my hair
I laughed and told him, "don't go there"

Refuse to take him to the east coast
I am not ashamed, but there I wouldn't boast

My hair breaks easily on counters and brushes
Shampoo squirts and conditioner gushes

Our children will have soft tresses to spare
It shouldn't matter – I shouldn't care

India Arie said I am not it
I think she was really on it

But I can't disguise my 4c
Chemicalize away the nappy

And the best part is that he loves me
Regardless of my crowning glory

Maybe It's Just Me

My friends are all artists
My friends are all magic
My friends are all crazy
Or maybe it's just me

My friends are all strong
My friends are all loyal
My friends are all weirdos
Or maybe it's me

My friends are all humble
My friends are all honest
My friends are all outrageous
Or maybe it's me

My friends are all mine
My friends are all growing
My friends are all with me
Lucky lucky me

Bravery
Dedicated to Kriss Mincey

Never so beautiful as when you are singing
And believe me young lady; you've got beauty in spades
But more than that
It is your bravery I most admire
It is the golden power in you
Your chocolate brown soul
That says
I can smile and sing
America can see me
The world can hear me
I am inspired by your bootstraps
The very ones you use to lift yourself up
Cute like the sandals I saw you wear one time
Or the song in the basement
I heard you croon
When you were giving thanks
And your smile tells stories, girl
Smart chic
Black nightingale
Tickle YOU love
Thursday night soul cries deep like music fingers
In the waves of oceans of ears
Fearless and fierce
Your bravery like an amulet
Your determination like a phalanx
You are a force
I am so humbled
And inspired too
Never so beautiful as when you are singing
And believe me young lady,
You've got beauty in spades

So Honored

I saw a smile today that lit me from inside
A warm fire of a thing
A secret untold
A kiss
Not yet given
A white dress
A warm hand
A loyal heart
I saw a smile today that lit me from inside
Despite myself
I burn hope
A touch
Promised to promise
To please
To protect
To honor
I saw a smile today that lit me from inside
A beautiful tear
Joy on the move
A child
Or perhaps, children
A clan
A truth
My own

I Look to You

I look to you
horizon
From this room in which I've hidden
From this lie to which I've listened
For so long

A little girl hearing voices
Telling her to trust no one
Telling her she's alone
But that's wrong

I look to you
horizon
For the beauty of my loved ones
For the friends who said now hold on
Their friendship proves God true

A little girl watching sunsets
For the beauty of the future
For the mending, healing sutures
And a trail of hope to pursue

Almost

I was sure of the magic almost
The spirit within the sensitive heart
That almost captivated my week
My month
My year
My life
Almost
I was sure of the destiny almost
The crown and the scepter
That almost stole me away to their kingdom Their land
Their house
Their parlor
Almost
I was sure of the rage almost
The fire burning beneath the stone
That burned the truth into my eyes
Into my hands
Into my life
Freedom is never
Almost
The silent war is over almost
The unforgiving nights and days
Until I finally forgave
Fully let be
Fully laid to rest
And let myself be at rest
Freedom is never
Almost

Worlds

There are so many different worlds around
I see how I am or am not a part
Each group, each grouping
It's amazing, our microcosms
Sometimes I just like standing from the outer atmosphere
Looking in
An alien
The world of the traveller at the airport
His uniform
Her gear
The world of the small-town family
Her peace
His release
The world of the...insert your own
SO many worlds
All around us
So many different worlds
Like jewels
Like joys
So many worlds around

~~~ ~~~ ~~~

Cuando me sueño, uso una lengua que es solo mio
Una sonrisa, una palabra, un cuerpo tambien
Mi corazon esta fuerte, mi boca es grande
Mi cabeza es el mar, mis manos son montañas
Un chiste de sangue y hueso
Yo soy mi sueño
Mi sueño de yo

In Transit

On your mark, get set, GO
Where though
A pioneer through life's paths
A journey from here to eternity
A wanderer through the wonder of the simplest moments
I am in transit
I am not easily surprised, but life has a way of shutting me up
The more I learn, the more I see, the more I wish for simple songs
and writing
The less I want to talk, the more I want to ask
What do you want to learn from your life?
What do you want to teach through your experiences?
What do you want your legacy to be?
Let's transit together and share the load
Let's converse about our wonder-wanders
And save each other time and trial
Learning to lean, learning to bow, learning to pray
As we travel from death to life
Let's enjoy the story
Show me your battle scars and I'll show you mine
From the past, when we were stupid
Yes, even five seconds ago
I am tired of my ears being tickled
We are moving from ignorance to wisdom
Through trial and text and a multitude of counsel
I want to go hard after life and excellence
So that when I am old my age will speak wisdom
I will tell my younger ones from experiences
And so I go, and I will bring stories in transit

Season

As if on the wind
As if from a kiss
I smell the perfected seedling
I sense great harvest
Yes, it is coming, that time

The death of a seed
Is not for mourning
The coming fruit shows us
Seeds die for the turning
Yes, it is coming, that time

The music of change
The joy of root taken
Through ground-breaking growth pain
For sickle and staking
Yes, it is coming, that time

Call it a journey
Or perhaps a process
Life through morbid shift
Such metamorphosis
Yes, it is coming, that time

The cycle is certain
Of death breeding life
Skulls are not the stopping point
But a stanza in rhyme
Yes, it is coming, that time

The turn of phrase
From Summer to Fall
To glean what was planted
Great reward from seed small
Yes, it is indeed coming, that time

Pondering

This is how I felt
like a gray day with the sun peeking out
This is what I was
A ball of confusion when you just start to see what it's about
It is a beautiful thing
the diamond unicorn's eye
Inside a kaleidoscope chamber
dying because it couldn't fly
This has become thus
The beauty of smart
Where repetitions fade
and verbal delicacies depart
Chewing now on multifaceted tastes
Beauty for knowledge
what a price to pay

At Any Age

Bottled potential
That's what they call me
Hope on copious amounts
of drugs

Scandalous hope
I dare you to stop me
I dare me
to keep going

Bottled potential
Shaken like soda
My limits are a Tetris
Fit into my future

You sir
Are in my way
Don't say
I didn't warn you

Bottled potential
That's what I exude
That's why I'm creating
That's how I'm here

Girl Thinks
For Shelby Lynne

Among the many shades and shadows
Of a woman's mind
Come the girl-thinks of days past
Experiences that have moulded and shaped current thoughts
They seep through
Weeds from when
She was young inside
Her girl-thinks have shaped
Many days and nights
Until she wondered if there ever would be
A new moment
A new girl-think
Something to shift her direction
From the playground to the future
Shifting girl-thinks
Because there are bigger concerns
Than that of a mere girl
As if she ever was
Just a mere girl
Lift healing hands to the woman
Trapped inside the girl-think
Trapped inside the womb
A womb of wonder
Wandering from girl to woman

For the Seiling Girls

Hey you, small town girl!
Ride your bike, wear your boots!
Hey you, small town girl!
Walk to church, the library, or school!
You know who you are
And you stand strong
Rodeo princess without a horse
Bringing smiles like corn ears all day long
Hey you, small town girl!
Take your Ag class, join 4H!
Hey you, small town girl!
Drive to Woodward, it's OK!
You were all the most glittering ladies
Each and every one
From ages seven to seventy
Your cadence good and strong

～～ ～～ ～～ ～～

The Contradiction

Her voice is so soft, it belies her strength
A strength forgotten in the many obstacles
I wish her power I cannot give
She must take it
She must fight her way to stay awake
Where do they go?
These with voices gone
She whispers
Echoes of beautiful power
Sex, sass, strength, sufficiency
I've lost her
She lost her
I'm not the map
I'm not the way back
But I know she must go back
Back home to her self

Two Weeks' Notice

If overthinking were a job
I was a Chief Administrative Officer
And hating my position
I had a beautiful office
In a beautiful building
In the middle of a storm
Of my own creation
And I loved and hated
My own mind
My beautiful mind
My mental self-weapon
But
I put in my two weeks' notice
I was not fired
Terminated for cause
I quit the job
So that my heart could beat
So that I could dream
So that I could love
So that I could create
And laugh and sing and dance
In the clear light of the sun

Weeding Word Weeds

A word weed, finding itself sacred, begs to overgrow and overthrow me. It's like being accosted by a thought, or worse a thought process that chokes the effervescence of creativity within me.

I don't want to be this weird. Please let me be normal. Says the word weed over and over. It tendrils and vines around my hopes, my art, myself.

In my efforts to remain unsullied, I find pruning this thought a constant. I find pulling down this thought process a necessity.

I am a song lyric. It wants me to be a sentence. I am lightning. It wants me to be a desk lamp. I am a torch. It wants me to be a match. I beg to break out of my own limitation. It begs me to be quieter, more afraid of what people will think.

In my efforts to remain unsullied, I tell myself I am worth the weeding, the pruning. I tell myself that this weed is beneath me, for all its toil.

A Letter

We hit the ground running, unafraid of the fall, the dirt, the ants or the flying things. The older we get the younger we become. Broken bones and scars mean more or perhaps just different things. Details backlog our brains as we grow older; shaping our kaleidoscope of life experience into shapes and shades we are familiar with, comfortable with—even if the construct is a lie on all sides. We lean on these walls as if we can make them into steel by force of will. And then the election campaigns start, and the kaleidoscope turns, as does the microcosmic view of where we buy our coffee, tea, eggs and fruit. As does how we seek our lovers and woo them to share our newly shaped gilded cage.

We gild it.

It being our outside world. It being our point of view. It being our destiny, which still is a-flying at us, full speed, like time. Time is a serial killer. A serial killer of the gilded gild of lies and fears and definitions we wrap around ourselves like a blanket on Christmas morning.

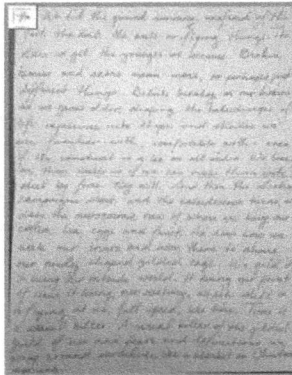

We Chased Dragons

We chased dragons into the sky
We gave them no quarter
In the desert
In the city
In our own minds
In politics
In social comments
In our bedrooms
In the mouths of others
And baring sword teeth and truth
We banned them from our hearts
We chased dragons into the sky
We gave them no quarter
We freed ourselves
In laughter
In touching
In forgiveness
In letting go
In hope
In joy
And baring sword teeth and truth
We banned them from our hearts
We chased dragons into the sky
We gave them no quarter

A Real Woman

To walk unbridled, without the restrictions of media or culture. To wear the clothes of freedom, and not of fashion. To taste the sweetness of teeth tailored to rip flesh, by brushing against them with my lips ever so gently. To *be* the force of nature, and not just feel it...

That is a real woman

To move when I please, and please when I move. To turn heads made of stone, and fill their bleak and empty existences with life and passion. To be more than just a vision of perfection to someone who does not know my flaws. To change at less than a moment's notice, and *expect* you to be ready. To make absolutely *no* sense, and understand why...

That is a real woman

To go forward, no matter the obstacle. To stand, no matter how wounded, and be a foundation, no matter how weary. To cradle your heart when the midnight is weeping. And to never see it as something one must do.

That is a real woman

Come with me and taste of my pleasures. Learn of my passions and pains. Join me in bliss- not knowing how, or where, or even why—only knowing that it is yours. Let me be for you what I truly am...

A real woman

A Woman but More

You recognize us easily enough,
and yet,
somehow,
you can't engage fully enough
not the womenfolk you think you found.
The damsels in suffocation have used intelligence as a weapon,
and Athena is reborn on the wet back of each female child.
Our magic is like water.
Yes it calms fires.
And yet it can burn with cold indifference.
Waves of anger may bury a town
just as the current of will may rebirth a nation.
As individuals we live by light of day,
and love by all hours.
In being ourselves,
we commune with heaven.
Our strategy is simple,
but unmatched.
We live, our purpose our own,
and you will never be able to resist it.

Too Strong to Bind

There really is nothing new under the sun
too strong to bind
you'll find...these preconceived notions
of beauty
of language
of danger and fear

There really is nothing new under the sun
too strong to bind
you'll find...these preconceived notions
of intellect
of communication
of security

this idea is unfinished...

Rehearsing Victories
Going Back from 2014

A year - Completed my Master's Thesis
Two years - Drove across the USA 1.5 times
Three years - Started graduate school
Four years - Went on a misadventure looking for Harriet Tubman's
house (I never found it)
Five years - Sang at Artscape
Six years - Drove in major snow for the first time
Seven years - Lived a song lyric – I got my "kicks on Route 66"
Eight years - Learned how to shoot .22's, build fire pits, and love
knives
Nine years - Sang in a Motown review band up and down the
California coast
Ten years – Pledged loyalty (with good reason) to my #1
restaurant for life - The Palace Grill, Santa Barbara
Eleven years - Wrote music for a Carillon (Played in UCSB's Storke
Tower)

Shall I keep making milestones?
Why, yes, I shall.

Time Capsule
Opened in 2013

You are beautiful.

You are smart.

"Stop seeing yourself through anyone's eyes but your own."

You are an artist.

You are a performer.

You drop pebbles in people so they can cause ripples...In themselves... in others. In you.

You are a Christchild. A queen. A priestess. Speak your sacred faith, child.

Now.

About the Author

Tiffany Vakilian called her mother one day in 2009, crying tears of joy and exclaiming, "I'm a writer Mom! I'm a writer!"

This was no surprise to her mother.

It was no surprise to her husband, who read one of her novellas on their first date. It was no surprise to her schoolmates at Goddard College, who asked her to MC the Open Mic every time she attended residency. It was no surprise to the band members when she came in with original songs for them to play in their jam sessions.

It certainly was no surprise to *A Word With You Press*, who published the book.

We hope you have enjoyed your brief visit into her talented mind, and that you join her again, next time she shares her world via words.

Guest Speaker

Tiffany Vakilian

www.speakfire.today

CEO and Founder of Speak Fire Publishing

Tiffany Vakilian is an entrepreneur with her Master's (and certification) in Transformative Language Arts. She is also an award-winning poet and performer committed to helping people use spoken, written, sung, or embodied word-art to facilitate social awareness and connection worldwide. Tiffany has a bold, yet tender style about her speaking that unlocks hidden stories within the audience, inspiring people to want to share those stories. She started SpeakFire Services to help unpublished authors go from holding their stories inside to confidently sharing polished, published books on the global stage.

Topics:

- *Need it, Want it, Deserve it* – Identity and Calling
- *Understanding Editing* – Technical Expertise with Inspiration
- *Back From the Dead* – The Power of Story

Great For:

- Keynotes
- Conferences
- Church Services
- Women's Retreats

Scan to schedule your **FREE** Author Breakthrough Session

Speak Fire Publishing

"STEP INTO YOUR FIRE WITH TIFFANY."

Dr. Jo Ann Pallay
"Dr. Jo"

TIFFANY VAKILIAN
619-292-8772
tiffany@speakfire.today